QUAIL FARMING

FOR BEGINNERS

THE ULTIMATE COMPREHENSIVE GUIDE

Copyright © 2023, Rachael B.

No part of this book may be reproduced or transmitted in any form or by any means, electronic or mechanical, including photocopying, recording, or by any information storage and retrieval system, without written permission from the copyright owner. All Rights Reserved

Disclaimer

The contents of this book are for the intention of those people intending to raise quail for a hobby. This book is written for informational purposes only. The author accepts no responsibility for any loss or consequential loss as a result of relying on any information or advice contained herein.

Copyright © 2023, Rachael B

All rights reserved

THANKS

I would like to thank all the quail keepers together with everyone I interacted with during the solicitation of information herein. Your guidance, corrections, hints and tips pointed me in the right direction. It's your invaluable inputs which made the publication of this book a reality.

DEDICATION

To Frank and Talia, you are my world

CONTENTS

QUAIL FARMING: INTRODUCTION..................................6

CHOOSING THE RIGHT QUAIL BREED............................9

SETTING UP A QUAIL FARMING OPERATION:
INFRASTRUCTURE AND EQUIPMENT..............................12

QUAIL HOUSING: OPTIONS AND CONSIDERATIONS........16

QUAIL NUTRITION: FEEDING AND WATERING YOUR
BIRDS 20

QUAIL BREEDING: STRATEGIES AND TECHNIQUES 23

INCUBATING AND HATCHING QUAIL EGGS 28

RAISING QUAIL CHICKS: CARE AND MANAGEMENT.......31

QUAIL HEALTH: COMMON DISEASES AND HOW TO
PREVENT THEM 36

QUAIL EGG PRODUCTION: MAXIMIZING YIELD 41

QUAIL MEAT PRODUCTION: MAXIMIZING YIELD 45

QUAIL EGG AND MEAT PROCESSING: TECHNIQUES AND
EQUIPMENT 47

QUAIL WASTE MANAGEMENT: HANDLING AND
COMPOSTING 52

MARKETING YOUR QUAIL PRODUCTS: FINDING CUSTOMERS AND BUILDING A BRAND **55**

TIPS AND TRICKS FOR SUCCESSFUL QUAIL FARMING **58**

CHAPTER 1

QUAIL FARMING: INTRODUCTION

Quail farming is a growing industry, offering small-scale farmers the opportunity to produce eggs and meat for local markets. Quail are small, hardy birds that are easy to raise and require less space and resources compared to other poultry.

In this comprehensive guide, we will cover all the basics of quail farming, from choosing the right quail breed and setting up your farm, to caring for your birds and maximizing production.

Before diving into the details, it's important to understand the basics of quail farming. Quail belong to the family of birds known as galliformes, which includes chickens, turkeys, and pheasants. There are several species of quail, but the most common ones used for farming are the Japanese quail and the Coturnix quail.

Quail are small birds, with adult males weighing around 7 ounces and females weighing around 6 ounces. They have a short lifespan of about 2-3 years and start laying eggs at around 6-8 weeks of age.

Quail eggs are smaller than chicken eggs, but they are high in protein and have a delicate, flavorful taste. Quail meat is also considered a delicacy, with a tender texture and a mild flavor.

Quail farming can be a lucrative business, as there is a growing demand for quail eggs and meat in many countries. Quail eggs are often used in gourmet dishes and are considered a health food due to their high protein and mineral content. Quail meat is also becoming more popular as a healthier alternative to chicken and other meats.

If you are considering starting a quail farm, there are a few things you should know. First, quail farming requires a relatively small investment compared to other types of poultry farming. Quail can be raised in small spaces, such as a backyard or a small farm, and they do not require expensive housing or equipment.

However, it's important to set up your farm properly to ensure the health and well-being of your birds.

Quail are easy to care for and do not require much attention. They are hardy birds that can withstand extreme weather conditions and are resistant to many common poultry diseases. However, it's important to provide your quail with a clean and well-ventilated environment and a healthy diet to ensure optimal growth and production.

In this guide, we will cover all the essential steps for starting and running a successful quail farm. We will discuss how to choose the right quail breed, set up your farm, care for your birds, and maximize production. With proper planning and management, quail farming can be a rewarding and profitable venture.

CHAPTER TWO

CHOOSING THE RIGHT QUAIL BREED

When it comes to starting a quail farm, choosing the right breed is an important decision. There are several different types of quail to choose from, each with their own unique characteristics and qualities. Here are some things to consider when selecting the right quail breed for your farm:

Egg production

Quail breeds that are known for their high egg production include the Japanese quail, the Bobwhite quail, and the Coturnix quail. These breeds can lay up to 300 eggs per year, making them a good choice for commercial egg production.

Meat production

If you are looking to raise quail for meat, you will want to choose a breed that grows quickly and has a good feed conversion ratio. Some good options for meat production include the Coturnix quail, the Jumbo Brown quail, and the Texas A&M quail. These breeds are known for their fast growth rate and high meat-to-bone ratio.

Size

Quail come in a range of sizes, from small breeds like the Button quail (which can weigh as little as 3 ounces) to larger breeds like the Jumbo Brown quail (which can weigh up to 16 ounces). Consider the space you have available on your farm and choose a breed that will be comfortable in those conditions.

Temperament

Some quail breeds are known for being more docile and easier to handle, while others can be more skittish and difficult to handle. For example, the Japanese quail and the Button quail are known for being calm and easy to handle, while the Bobwhite quail can be more flighty and difficult to handle.

Consider your experience level and the amount of time you are willing to spend working with your quail when choosing a breed.

Climate

Different quail breeds are adapted to thrive in different climates. For example, the Button quail is well-suited to hot, humid environments, while the Bobwhite quail is more adapted to cooler climates. Choose a breed that will be comfortable in the climate you live in.

Appearance

Quail come in a variety of colors and patterns, including solid colors like white, brown, and black, as well as patterned feathers like speckled, barred, and laced. Consider the appearance of the quail when choosing a breed, but keep in mind that this should not be the primary factor in your decision.

Overall, it's important to do your research and consider all of these factors when choosing the right quail breed for your farm. Different breeds have different strengths and may be better suited to different goals and environments.

CHAPTER THREE

SETTING UP A QUAIL FARMING OPERATION: INFRASTRUCTURE AND EQUIPMENT

Starting a quail farming operation requires careful planning and consideration of various factors such as the location, infrastructure, and equipment needed. Here are some key points to consider when setting up a quail farm:

Building the quail house

The quail house should be designed to provide a comfortable and secure environment for the quails. This includes ensuring that the house is properly ventilated to prevent the build-up of ammonia and other harmful gases, and that it has proper lighting to support the quails' growth and development. The quail house should also have a temperature control system to keep the quails at a comfortable temperature.

Flooring material:

The flooring material in the quail house should be easy to clean and disinfect to prevent the spread of diseases. Some options include concrete, wood shavings, or straw. It is important to regularly clean and disinfect the flooring to maintain a healthy environment for the quails.

Feeders and waterers

Quails need access to feed and water at all times, so it is important to invest in high-quality feeders and waterers. These should be designed to prevent the feed and water from becoming contaminated and to make it easy for the quails to access. It is also a good idea to have multiple feeders and waterers to ensure that all of the quails have access to food and water.

Incubators

Incubators are essential for hatching quail eggs. It is important to choose an incubator that is capable of maintaining a consistent temperature and humidity level to support the development of the embryos. The incubator should also have a turning mechanism to ensure that the eggs are turned regularly, as this is essential for proper development.

Egg trays

Egg trays are used to collect and store the quail eggs until they are ready to be sold. It is important to choose egg trays that are sturdy and able to support the weight of the eggs without crushing them. Egg trays should also be designed to prevent the eggs from rolling around and potentially cracking.

Chick brooder

A chick brooder is a small enclosure that is used to keep young quails warm and comfortable during their first few weeks of life. It is important to choose a chick brooder that is large enough to accommodate the number of quails being raised and that has a heat source to keep the quails warm. The chick brooder should also have a bedding material such as wood shavings or straw to provide a comfortable surface for the quails to rest on.

Weighing scale

A weighing scale is used to accurately measure the weight of the quail eggs and meat. This is important for pricing the quail products and for monitoring the growth and development of the quails.

Candling lamp

A candling lamp is a tool that is used to examine the inside of a quail egg without breaking it open. This is done by shining a light through the egg and observing the inside. Candling lamps are used to assess the quality of the eggs and to identify any problems such as abnormalities or signs of infection.

Cooling system

A cooling system is necessary to keep the quail eggs fresh and prevent them from spoiling. There are several options for cooling the eggs, including refrigeration units or cooling rooms with fans.

It is important to choose a cooling system that is capable of maintaining a consistent temperature to ensure that the eggs are stored at the optimal temperature.

Managing the quails

Quails require a balanced diet and regular care to maintain their health. It is important to provide them with a high-quality feed that is formulated specifically for quails. The feed should be supplemented with additional nutrients such as vitamins and minerals to ensure that the quails are getting all the nutrients they need. Quails also need to have access to clean water at all times.

Marketing the quail products

Once the quail farming operation is up and running, it is important to establish a marketing plan to sell the quail eggs and meat. This can include establishing relationships with local restaurants and grocery stores, or selling the products directly to consumers through farmers markets or online platforms.

Overall, setting up a quail farming operation requires careful planning and a commitment to providing the best possible care for the quails. By investing in the right infrastructure and equipment and managing the quails effectively, it is possible to successfully operate a quail farm and provide a high-quality product to the market.

CHAPTER FOUR

QUAIL HOUSING: OPTIONS AND CONSIDERATIONS

Quail housing is an essential aspect of quail farming, as it plays a significant role in the health and productivity of the birds. There are several options to consider when it comes to quail housing, and it is important to carefully evaluate the pros and cons of each option to determine the best fit for your farm.

One option for quail housing is to use **a traditional poultry house**. These houses are typically made of wood or metal, and can be modified to meet the specific needs of quail.

Quail can be housed in cages or floor pens within the poultry house, and the size of the cages or pens should be carefully considered to ensure the birds have adequate space to move and forage.

It is generally recommended to provide at least 0.5 square feet of space per quail in a cage or pen, and at least 1 square foot per quail for floor pens. However, these are minimum recommendations, and it is generally recommended to provide more space if possible to promote the health and well-being of the birds.

In addition to the size of the cages or pens, it is important to ensure proper ventilation and access to natural light in the poultry house. Quail require a well-ventilated environment to maintain their health, and they also benefit from access to natural light, which can help regulate their sleep and feeding patterns.

One way to provide proper ventilation in a poultry house is to install fans or use natural ventilation through the use of windows or vents. It is also important to ensure that the poultry house is properly insulated to maintain a comfortable temperature for the quail, particularly in extreme weather conditions.

Another option for quail housing is to use **a mobile housing system, such as a chicken tractor or movable coop.** These systems allow for the quail to have access to fresh grass and forage, and can be moved to a new location on a regular basis to prevent overgrazing.

Mobile housing systems can be a good choice for smaller operations, as they allow for a more natural environment for the quail and can be less expensive to set up compared to a traditional poultry house.

However, mobile housing systems may not provide the same level of protection from predators as a traditional poultry house, and they may not be suitable for all climates or weather conditions.

It is important to carefully consider the size and design of a mobile housing system to ensure that it meets the needs of the quail. The size of the system should provide adequate space for the quail to move and forage, and it should also be sturdy and well-constructed to protect the birds from predators and the elements.

A third option for quail housing is **a high-density aviary system.** These systems use vertically stacked cages or pens, which can greatly increase the number of quail that can be housed in a given space.

High-density aviary systems can be a good choice for smaller operations, as they allow for a higher number of quail to be housed in a smaller space.However, these systems can be more expensive to set up and may require more labor to maintain, as the quail must be cared for and fed on a more individualized basis.

It is important to carefully consider the size and design of the cages or pens in a high-density aviary system, as the quail will need adequate space to move and forage.

When it comes to quail housing, it is important to consider the needs and behavior of the birds. Quail need access to clean water and feed, as well as a safe and comfortable environment.

They also need adequate space to move and forage, as well as access to natural light and proper ventilation.

CHAPTER FIVE

QUAIL NUTRITION: FEEDING AND WATERING YOUR BIRDS

Proper nutrition is essential for the health and well-being of quail. In this chapter, we will discuss the feeding and watering needs of quail, including the types of feed and supplements that are suitable for them.

Quail require a balanced diet that includes a variety of nutrients, including proteins, carbohydrates, fats, vitamins, and minerals. The specific nutritional requirements of quail vary depending on their age and stage of development. For example, quail chicks have different nutritional needs than adult quail.

One of the most important components of a quail's diet is protein. Quail require a high-protein feed, with a minimum of 18% protein for adult birds and 21% protein for growing chicks.

Good sources of protein for quail include grains, seeds, and legumes. Quail also require a source of carbohydrates, such as grains and seeds, for energy.

In addition to a balanced diet, quail also benefit from the addition of supplements. Calcium is an important supplement for quail, as it helps to strengthen their bones and eggshells. Quail can obtain calcium from crushed eggshells or a calcium supplement, such as oyster shell.

Other supplements that may be beneficial for quail include grit, which aids in digestion, and a vitamin and mineral supplement.

It is important to provide quail with a constant supply of fresh, clean water. Water is essential for quail to maintain proper hydration and to help them absorb nutrients from their food. Quail should have access to a clean, shallow water dish at all times.

It is also a good idea to provide a separate water dish for chicks, as their smaller beaks can make it difficult for them to access water in a deeper dish.

In summary, proper nutrition is essential for the health and well-being of quail. A balanced diet that includes a source of protein, carbohydrates, and supplements such as calcium and grit is important for quail of all ages.

Quail also require a constant supply of clean, fresh water. By providing your quail with proper nutrition and hydration, you can help them thrive and live a long, healthy life.

CHAPTER SIX

QUAIL BREEDING: STRATEGIES AND TECHNIQUES

Quail breeding can be a rewarding and exciting hobby, but it requires careful planning and attention to detail to be successful. Here are some strategies and techniques for successful quail breeding:

Choose the right breed

There are many different breeds of quail to choose from, each with its own unique characteristics. Some breeds, like the Japanese Quail, are known for their high egg production and are commonly used in commercial egg production. They can lay up to 300 eggs per year and are also popular as pets due to their small size and calm disposition. Other breeds, like the Bobwhite Quail, are popular for their meat and are often raised by hobbyists or small farmers. They are larger than Japanese Quails and have a more active and energetic personality.

When choosing a breed, consider your goals and the resources you have available. If you're interested in quail eggs, choose a breed that is known for its high egg production. If you're interested in quail meat, choose a breed that grows quickly and has a good meat-to-bone ratio.

It's also a good idea to research the specific care requirements of different breeds, as some may be more demanding in terms of space or diet than others.

Set up a suitable breeding environment

Quail need a clean, comfortable environment to thrive. A breeding pen or aviary that is at least 4 square feet per quail is recommended to give them enough space to move around and forage. The enclosure should be well-ventilated to prevent the buildup of harmful gases and moisture, and it should be temperature-controlled to keep the quail comfortable. A quail house or chicken coop can be modified to create a suitable breeding environment, or you can build a custom enclosure to meet your specific needs.

It's important to keep the breeding environment clean to prevent the spread of disease. Quail produce a lot of droppings, so the enclosure should be cleaned regularly to remove excess manure and prevent the buildup of ammonia gas, which can be harmful to the birds' respiratory system.

Provide a nutritious diet

Quail need a balanced diet to stay healthy and productive. A commercial quail feed that is formulated specifically for breeding quail should be the mainstay of their diet, and it should be supplemented with fresh greens and other protein sources like mealworms or crickets. Quail also need a constant supply of clean water, so make sure to provide clean water bottles or a water dish that can't be tipped over.

Keep track of your birds' health

Regularly check your quail for signs of illness, such as sneezing, lethargy, or diarrhea. Quail are prone to respiratory infections and parasites, so it's important to keep their environment clean and free of any potential sources of contamination. If you notice any unusual symptoms, isolate the affected quail and consult a veterinarian or a poultry specialist for treatment.

Select the best breeding pairs

Quail breeding success depends on choosing the right breeding pairs. Look for birds that are healthy, of good size and conformation, and have a good egg production history. Avoid breeding birds that are related, as this can lead to genetic defects. It's also a good idea to select breeding pairs that have compatible personalities, as quail can be prone to aggression if they are not compatible.

Incubate eggs properly

Quail eggs can be incubated using either a commercial incubator or a homemade set-up. If you're using a commercial incubator, follow the manufacturer's instructions for temperature and humidity settings. If you're using a homemade incubator, it's important to maintain a constant temperature of 99-100 degrees Fahrenheit and a humidity level of around 50%. The eggs should also be turned regularly to ensure proper development.

Raise the chicks properly

Quail chicks are very delicate and require special care. Keep them in a brooder with a heat lamp to provide a warm, consistent temperature, and offer a starter feed that is formulated specifically for quail chicks. As they grow, gradually introduce them to a more varied diet and larger living space. Make sure to provide plenty of clean water and keep the brooder clean to prevent the spread of disease.

As the chicks grow, they will need more space to move around and explore. A quail pen or aviary that is at least 4 square feet per bird is recommended to give them enough room to move and forage. Gradually acclimate the chicks to the outdoor environment by allowing them access to a small outdoor run or enclosure.

By following these strategies and techniques, you can set yourself up for success in quail breeding and enjoy the rewards of raising healthy, productive birds. It's important to be patient and stay committed to the process, as quail breeding can require a lot of time and attention. With proper care and planning, however, you can experience the joy of raising and breeding these fascinating and rewarding birds.

CHAPTER SEVEN

INCUBATING AND HATCHING QUAIL EGGS

Incubating and hatching quail eggs can be a fun and rewarding experience for those interested in raising their own quails.

Incubator Selection

When choosing an incubator for quail eggs, it's important to select one that is specifically designed for small eggs. Quail eggs are much smaller than chicken eggs, and an incubator that is too large or has too much airflow can result in low hatch rates.

It's also a good idea to choose an incubator that has a built-in thermostat and humidity control, as maintaining the proper temperature and humidity levels is crucial for successful incubation.

Incubation Process

Once the incubator is set up and the eggs have been placed inside, it's important to monitor the temperature and humidity levels closely. Quail eggs require a temperature of 99-100°F and a humidity level of 50-55%. These levels can be maintained by using a thermometer and hygrometer to measure the temperature and humidity and adjusting the incubator accordingly. The eggs should also be turned several times a day, with the small end pointing down and the large end pointing up, to ensure proper circulation of air and nutrients.

Candling

Candling is a technique used to check the fertility of quail eggs and assess the progress of incubation. It involves holding the egg up to a bright light or using a small flashlight to shine through the shell. A fertile egg will have a small, dark spot at the center, called the blastoderm, which will eventually develop into the embryo. Candling can be done at several points during the incubation process, but it is most commonly done at 7-10 days to check for fertility and again at 18-21 days to check for hatching.

Hatching

After 18-21 days of incubation, the eggs should start to hatch. The hatching process can take several hours, and the chicks will use their egg tooth, a small, sharp bump on the top of their beak, to break through the shell. It's important to monitor the hatching process closely and remove the chicks from the incubator as soon as they hatch to prevent them from getting too cold or becoming distressed.

Brooding

Once the chicks have hatched, they should be removed from the incubator and placed in a brooder, which is a small, enclosed area designed for raising young poultry. The brooder should have a heat source, such as a heat lamp or heating pad, to keep the chicks warm, as well as a supply of clean water and a starter feed formulated for quail. As the chicks grow, they can be gradually transitioned to a grower feed and given access to an outdoor run or pen.

Raising Quail

Raising quail can be a rewarding experience, and these small birds are easy to care for and require minimal space. They are also a great source of fresh eggs and meat. With proper care and attention, you can successfully raise a healthy, happy flock of quail in your backyard.

CHAPTER EIGHT

RAISING QUAIL CHICKS: CARE AND MANAGEMENT

Housing

The brooder should be large enough to allow the chicks to move around and explore, but not so large that they get chilled. A general rule of thumb is to provide at least 0.5 square feet of space per chick.

The floor of the brooder should be covered with a soft material, such as straw or shredded paper, to provide insulation and prevent leg problems.

It is important to provide enough ventilation to prevent the buildup of ammonia from the chicks' waste. This can be achieved by using a mesh wire top or by installing windows or vents.

To provide heat, you can use a heat lamp or infrared bulb mounted at one end of the brooder. The heat source should be positioned so that the chicks can move away from it if they get too warm.

A thermometer should be used to monitor the temperature of the brooder, and the heat source should be adjusted accordingly to maintain the appropriate temperature.

As the chicks grow and feather out, the temperature of the brooder can be gradually reduced by 5 degrees each week.

Feed and water

Quail chicks should be fed a starter feed that is specifically formulated for their needs. The feed should contain a minimum of 20% protein and should be supplemented with grit and calcium to support the development of strong bones.

The feed should be offered in a shallow dish or trough, and the chicks should have access to clean water at all times.

The water should be changed daily to prevent contamination, and a water heater can be used to keep the water at the appropriate temperature in cold weather.

As the chicks grow, they can be transitioned to a grower or finisher feed, depending on their age and size. It is important to follow the recommended feeding guidelines for the specific feed you are using.

Health and hygiene

Quail chicks are susceptible to a variety of health issues, including respiratory infections, parasites, and leg problems. It is important to monitor the chicks for any signs of illness, such as coughing, sneezing, lethargy, or diarrhea.

If you notice any signs of illness, it is important to consult a veterinarian as soon as possible. Your veterinarian can diagnose the problem and provide treatment recommendations.

To prevent the spread of disease, it is important to keep the brooder clean and disinfected. The floor should be cleaned and bedding should be replaced as needed. Any sick chicks should be isolated from the rest of the flock to prevent the spread of illness.

It is also important to practice good biosecurity measures, such as washing your hands before handling the chicks and keeping the brooder isolated from other animals and birds.

Socialization

Quail chicks are social animals and should be handled regularly to encourage bonding and prevent aggression. Handling the chicks can also help to tame them and make them more comfortable around humans.

It is also important to introduce quail chicks to other birds and animals at a young age to prevent fear and aggression later on. This can be done by allowing the chicks to interact with other birds or animals under supervision, or by exposing them to different sights, sounds, and smells.

Growth and development

Quail chicks grow rapidly and should be monitored for proper development. The chicks should reach their adult size at about 6-8 weeks of age, and their wings should be trimmed at this time to prevent flying.

Quail chicks can begin laying eggs at around 16 weeks of age, although this will depend on the specific breed and individual bird. Some breeds

Some breeds of quail, such as Japanese quail, can start laying eggs as early as 8 weeks of age, while other breeds, such as Coturnix quail, may take longer to mature. It is important to research the specific breed you are raising to understand their expected growth and development timeline.

As the chicks grow and reach laying age, they will need to be transitioned to a laying diet that is higher in protein and calcium to support egg production.

It is also important to provide the quail with appropriate nesting boxes and substrate, such as straw or wood shavings, to encourage egg laying.

Handling and transportation

Quail chicks should be handled gently and with care to prevent injury. It is important to support their head and body when picking them up, and to handle them as little as possible to prevent stress.

When transporting quail chicks, it is important to use a secure and well-ventilated container to prevent stress and injury. The container should be large enough to allow the chicks to move around, but not so large that they get chilled.

It is also important to consider the temperature and weather when transporting quail chicks, and to take appropriate measures to keep them warm and protected.

In summary, raising quail chicks requires a commitment to proper housing, nutrition, health care, and socialization. By following these guidelines, you can ensure that your quail chicks grow up to be healthy and well-adjusted birds. Proper care and management is essential for the success of any quail breeding operation, and by taking the time to properly care for your chicks, you can raise healthy and productive birds that will provide you with enjoyment and potentially even a source of income.

CHAPTER NINE

QUAIL HEALTH: COMMON DISEASES AND HOW TO PREVENT THEM

Respiratory Disease

Respiratory disease in quail is often caused by poor ventilation, crowded conditions, and exposure to cold temperatures. It can also be caused by bacteria or viruses, such as Mycoplasma or avian influenza. Some common signs of respiratory disease in quail include coughing, sneezing, nasal discharge, and difficulty breathing. In severe cases, it can lead to lethargy, weight loss, and even death.

To prevent respiratory disease, it is important to provide your quail with plenty of fresh air and a dry, well-ventilated environment. Quail need a minimum of 1 square foot of ventilation per bird, so be sure to provide enough windows, vents, or exhaust fans to meet this requirement. It is also a good idea to avoid overcrowding your quail, as this can lead to poor air quality and an increased risk of respiratory disease. Aim for at least 4-6 square feet of space per bird, depending on the size of your quail and the type of housing you are using.

In addition to proper ventilation, it is important to keep your quail warm and protected from drafts. Quail are sensitive to cold temperatures and can easily succumb to respiratory illness if exposed to cold drafts or wet conditions. To keep your quail warm and dry, consider using a heat lamp or heater in the winter, and make sure to keep their bedding dry and free of moisture.

Coccidiosis

Coccidiosis is a parasitic disease caused by a protozoan parasite called coccidia, which can be transmitted through contaminated feed, water, or soil. It affects the intestinal tract of quail, leading to symptoms such as diarrhea, weight loss, and lethargy. In severe cases, it can lead to dehydration and death.

To prevent coccidiosis, it is important to keep your quail's housing clean and to provide them with clean, fresh water and feed. This will help to reduce the risk of contamination with the coccidia parasite. It is also a good idea to regularly deworm your quail, as this can help to reduce the number of coccidia present in the intestinal tract. In addition, you can use a coccidiostat in their feed to prevent the development of the parasite. Coccidiostats are medications that kill coccidia and help to prevent coccidiosis in quail.

Mites and Lice

Mites and lice are common parasites that can affect quail, causing irritation and discomfort. Mites and lice can be transmitted through contact with other birds or by coming into contact with contaminated equipment or bedding. Some signs of mites or lice infestation include excessive scratching, feather loss, and thinning of the feathers. In severe cases, it can lead to anemia and death.

To prevent mites and lice, it is important to keep your quail's housing clean and to regularly check for signs of infestation. This includes inspecting your quail's feathers and skin for mites and lice, as well as checking their bedding and equipment for the presence of these pests. If you do find mites or lice, it is important to treat them promptly to prevent the infestation from spreading.

There are several products available for the treatment of mites and lice in quail, including dusts, sprays, and medications. Be sure to follow the manufacturer's instructions carefully when using any of these products.

Leg Problems

Leg problems, such as sprains and fractures, are common health issues affecting quails. Leg problems in quail can be caused by a variety of factors, including overcrowding, rough terrain, and improper nutrition. Quail have small, delicate legs that can be easily injured if they are not provided with a smooth and even floor surface. To prevent leg problems, it is important to provide your quail with plenty of space and a smooth, even floor surface. Aim for at least 4-6 square feet of space per bird, depending on the size of your quail and the type of housing you are using.

In addition to proper space and flooring, it is important to provide your quail with a balanced diet. Quail need a diet that is high in protein and calcium to support their growth and development. A lack of these nutrients can lead to weak bones and an increased risk of leg problems. Be sure to provide your quail with a commercial quail feed that is formulated for their specific needs, or consider supplementing their diet with high-quality protein and calcium sources, such as leafy greens, seeds, and grains.

Eye Problems

Eye problems, such as conjunctivitis, are another common health issue among quail. Eye problems can be caused by a variety of factors, including infection, injury, and allergies. Some signs of eye problems in quail include redness, swelling, discharge, and squinting. In severe cases, it can lead to blindness.

To prevent eye problems, it is important to keep your quail's housing clean and to provide them with fresh, uncontaminated water. It is also a good idea to regularly check your quail's eyes for any signs of infection or injury, and to seek veterinary care if necessary. If you are using any medications or treatments on your quail, be sure to follow the manufacturer's instructions carefully to avoid causing any eye irritation or damage.

Overall, the key to maintaining the health of your quail is to provide them with a clean, well-ventilated environment, plenty of space, and a balanced diet. By following these simple guidelines, you can help keep your quail happy and healthy for years to come.

CHAPTER TEN

QUAIL EGG PRODUCTION: MAXIMIZING YIELD

Quail egg production has gained popularity in recent years due to the high demand for these delicacies and their numerous health benefits. Quail eggs are rich in vitamins, minerals, and protein, making them a nutritious addition to any diet. Additionally, they have a delicate and unique flavor that sets them apart from chicken eggs.

There are several factors that can influence the yield of a quail egg production operation. Proper management and attention to detail are crucial to maximizing the number of eggs produced. Here are some tips to help you get the most out of your quail egg production:

Selecting the right breed

In addition to considering the egg-laying capabilities of different quail breeds, it is also important to consider their size and overall suitability for your operation. For example, if you have limited space, you may want to choose a smaller breed that can be housed in a smaller coop. It is also worth considering the climate of your location, as some breeds may be better suited to certain environments. Researching and carefully selecting the right breed for your operation can help ensure that you get the most out of your quail egg production.

Providing a suitable environment

The housing for your quail should be spacious enough to allow them to move around freely, with adequate ventilation to prevent the buildup of harmful gases. The coop should also be protected from extreme weather conditions, such as extreme heat or cold, to ensure the comfort of your birds. In addition to temperature and humidity control, the coop should also provide plenty of natural light, as this can help stimulate egg production in quail.

Implementing a consistent routine

Quail are sensitive to changes in their environment and routine, and this can cause stress that can impact their egg production. To prevent this, it is important to establish a consistent routine for your birds, including regular feedings, clean water, and a consistent light cycle. This can help reduce stress and improve the overall health and egg-laying rate of your quail.

Monitoring your birds' health

Regularly checking the health of your quail is crucial to maintaining a high egg production rate. This includes looking for signs of illness, such as lethargy, loss of appetite, or diarrhea, and taking corrective action if necessary. It is also important to keep the coop clean and free of any potential sources of disease, such as contaminated feed or water.

Using supplements

Adding supplements to the diet of your quail can help improve egg production by providing them with the nutrients they need to lay eggs. Calcium, in particular, is important for the development of strong eggshells. Vitamin D can also help improve egg production by aiding in the absorption of calcium. It is important to carefully follow the recommended dosage of any supplements you provide to your quail, as over-supplementation can have negative consequences.

Practicing good hygiene

Good hygiene is essential in any egg production operation to ensure the quality and safety of the eggs. This includes regularly cleaning the coop and equipment, providing clean water and feed, and separating sick birds from the rest of the flock to prevent the spread of disease. It is also important to handle the eggs with care and to follow proper washing and sanitation procedures to prevent contamination.

In conclusion, maximizing quail egg production requires a combination of proper management, a suitable environment, and attention to the needs of the birds. By following these tips and paying attention to the details of your quail egg production operation, you can maximize the yield of your quail and enjoy the delicious and nutritious rewards of these delicate eggs.

CHAPTER ELEVEN

QUAIL MEAT PRODUCTION: MAXIMIZING YIELD

Quail meat production can be maximized through several strategies, including breeding for high-yield traits, proper feeding and nutrition, and efficient management practices.

Breeding for high-yield traits

In addition to selecting quail strains with good growth rate and feed conversion efficiency, it may also be helpful to implement a breeding program that emphasizes these traits. This may involve crossing quail with high-yield genetics and selecting the offspring with the best traits for breeding. It can also be helpful to track the performance of individual birds and use this information to make informed breeding decisions.

Proper feeding and nutrition

A balanced diet is essential for quail to reach their maximum weight and meat yield. This may include a commercial quail feed that is formulated to meet their specific nutritional needs. Quail require a high protein diet, so it may also be helpful to supplement their diet with protein sources such as soybeans, fishmeal, or insects. In addition to the right nutrients, it is also important to provide quail with access to clean, fresh water at all times.

Efficient management practices

Proper housing and sanitation are essential for maximizing meat production. Quail should be housed in a clean, well-ventilated facility that is free of pests and diseases. Regular monitoring and health care are also important, as quail are susceptible to a variety of illnesses that can affect their growth and overall health. This may include providing preventive care such as vaccinations and implementing strategies to minimize stress and maintain a healthy environment.

Overall, maximizing quail meat production requires a combination of careful planning and attention to detail. By implementing strategies such as breeding for high-yield traits, providing proper feeding and nutrition, and practicing efficient management, it is possible to increase meat production and improve the profitability of a quail meat operation.

CHAPTER TWELVE

QUAIL EGG AND MEAT PROCESSING: TECHNIQUES AND EQUIPMENT

Quail eggs and meat are becoming increasingly popular in the culinary world due to their delicate flavor and numerous health benefits. As a result, there is a growing demand for quail egg and meat processing techniques and equipment.

There are several methods for processing quail eggs, including hard boiling, soft boiling, pickling, and frying. Hard boiling quail eggs involves placing the eggs in a pot of boiling water for 6-8 minutes, then transferring them to an ice bath to cool before peeling. Soft boiling quail eggs involves cooking them for a shorter amount of time, typically 3-4 minutes, resulting in a softer yolk and a semi-solid white. Pickling quail eggs involves soaking them in a vinegar-based brine for several days to a week, resulting in a tangy and slightly sour flavor. Frying quail eggs involves coating them in beaten egg and breadcrumbs or flour, then pan frying them until the whites are set and the yolks are cooked to the desired degree of doneness.

Quail meat too can be processed using a variety of techniques, including roasting, grilling, frying, and braising. Roasting quail involves cooking the birds in the oven at a high temperature, resulting in a crispy skin and moist meat.

Grilling quail involves cooking the birds over a bed of hot coals or a gas flame, resulting in a smoky flavor and charred exterior. Frying quail involves coating the birds in flour or breadcrumbs and pan frying them in hot oil until the exterior is crispy and the meat is cooked through. Braising quail involves cooking the birds in a liquid, such as stock or wine, at a low temperature for an extended period of time, resulting in tender, fall-off-the-bone meat.

One important aspect of quail egg processing is proper handling and storage. Fresh quail eggs should be handled with care to prevent cracking or damaging the shells. It is important to store quail eggs in a clean, dry place at a consistent temperature, as fluctuations in temperature can cause the eggs to spoil more quickly. Quail eggs can be stored in the refrigerator for up to a week, or they can be frozen for longer-term storage. When freezing quail eggs, it is important to crack the eggs and mix the whites and yolks together before freezing, as the yolks will become gummy if frozen whole.

Equipment

In terms of equipment, there are a few key items that are essential for quail egg processing. One important tool is an egg topper, which is used to neatly cut the tops off of hard boiled quail eggs. An egg topper typically consists of a small, sharp blade that can be pressed down onto the top of the egg to cut a circular shape out of the shell. This allows the top of the egg to be easily removed, revealing the fully cooked yolk and white inside.

Another essential piece of equipment for quail egg processing is an egg grader. This machine is used to sort quail eggs by size, as quail eggs can vary in size even within a single clutch. An egg grader typically consists of a series of sloping ramps or chutes, along with a series of holes or openings of different sizes. The eggs are placed on the ramps or chutes and roll down under the influence of gravity, falling through the holes or openings that match their size. The graded eggs are then collected in separate bins or trays according to size.

In addition to these specialized tools, there are also a number of more general-purpose pieces of equipment that are commonly used in quail egg processing. For example, pots and pans are essential for boiling and frying quail eggs, and a variety of utensils, such as spatulas and tongs, can be useful for handling the eggs during cooking. Other important items include bowls for mixing ingredients, measuring cups and spoons for precise measurements, and food thermometers for ensuring that the eggs are cooked to the proper temperature.

For quail meat processing, there are also a number of specialized tools and equipment that can be used. One important piece of equipment is a meat slicer, which is used to slice quail meat into thin, uniform slices. A meat slicer typically consists of a sharp blade mounted on a sliding carriage, which can be adjusted to achieve the desired thickness of the slices. This can be particularly useful for preparing quail meat for sandwiches or other dishes where thin, even slices are desired.

Other important pieces of equipment for quail meat processing include knives and cutting boards for preparing the meat, and a variety of pots, pans, and roasting pans for cooking the meat. A meat thermometer is also essential for ensuring that the quail meat is cooked to the proper temperature, as undercooking or overcooking can result in a subpar final product.

In addition to these basic tools, there are also more advanced pieces of equipment that can be used in quail meat processing. For example, some processors use machines to debone quail meat, which can be a time-consuming and labor-intensive process when done by hand. There are also machines available for tenderizing quail meat, which can help to make it more flavorful and easier to chew. Finally, there are packaging and labeling machines that can be used to package and label the finished quail meat products, making them ready for sale.

Overall, the techniques and equipment used for quail egg and meat processing vary depending on the specific method of preparation and the desired end result. However, the use of high-quality, specialized equipment can help to ensure consistent results and maximize efficiency in the processing of these delicate and flavorful products.

CHAPTER THIRTEEN

QUAIL WASTE MANAGEMENT: HANDLING AND COMPOSTING

Proper quail waste management is an important aspect of quail farming and processing. Quail produce a variety of waste materials, including manure, feathers, and eggshells, which must be properly handled and disposed of to minimize environmental impacts and prevent the spread of disease.

One common method of quail waste management is composting. Composting involves the decomposition of organic materials, such as manure and feathers, through the action of microorganisms. When properly managed, composting can convert quail waste into a nutrient-rich soil amendment that can be used to improve the fertility of agricultural land.

To compost quail waste, it is important to follow a few basic guidelines. First, the compost pile should be located in a well-draining area with good airflow to promote the growth of microorganisms. The pile should also be kept moist, but not waterlogged, to support the decomposition process. It is also important to regularly turn the compost pile to provide oxygen to the microorganisms and ensure that the waste materials are properly decomposed.

In addition to quail manure and feathers, eggshells can also be composted. Eggshells are high in calcium, which can be beneficial to plants. To compost eggshells, they should be crushed or ground into a fine powder before being added to the compost pile. This helps to speed up the decomposition process and ensure that the eggshells are properly integrated into the compost.

Another important aspect of quail waste management is the handling of dead birds. Quail, like all animals, will occasionally die due to illness or old age. It is important to properly dispose of dead birds to prevent the spread of disease and minimize the risk of infection to other quail. There are a few different methods for disposing of dead quail, including burial, incineration, and rendering.

Burial is a simple and effective method for disposing of dead quail, although it may not be practical in areas where the ground is frozen or hard. To bury quail, the birds should be placed in a biodegradable bag or container and buried at least three feet deep to prevent scavengers from digging them up.

Incineration is another option for disposing of dead quail. Incineration involves burning the birds to reduce them to ash, which can then be safely disposed of. This method is typically only practical for small numbers of dead quail, as it requires specialized equipment and may not be cost-effective for larger operations.

Rendering is a process that involves breaking down dead animals into their basic components, such as proteins and fats. The resulting materials can then be used as ingredients in a variety of products, including feed, fertilizers, and soap. Rendering is typically performed by specialized companies, and is a more costly option for disposing of dead quail compared to burial or incineration.

Overall, quail waste management is an important aspect of quail farming and processing. Proper handling and disposal of quail waste can help to minimize environmental impacts and prevent the spread of disease. By using composting and other methods, it is possible to effectively manage quail waste and turn it into a valuable resource.

CHAPTER FOURTEEN

MARKETING YOUR QUAIL PRODUCTS: FINDING CUSTOMERS AND BUILDING A BRAND

Marketing your quail products can be a challenging but rewarding task. It involves finding customers, building a brand, and ultimately, increasing sales. In this chapter, we will explore various strategies and techniques that you can use to effectively market your quail products and grow your business.

First and foremost, it is important to have a clear understanding of your target market. Who are the people that are most likely to be interested in your quail products? Are they health-conscious individuals who are looking for alternative protein sources? Are they foodies who are interested in trying new and unique flavors? Understanding your target market will help you tailor your marketing efforts and make them more effective.

One way to reach your target market is through social media marketing. With platforms like Facebook, Instagram, and Twitter, you can easily connect with potential customers and showcase your quail products. Use visually appealing photos and videos to highlight the unique qualities of your products and engage with your followers by asking for feedback and responding to comments and questions. You can also use social media to announce sales, promotions, and other special events.

Another effective marketing strategy is content marketing. This involves creating and sharing valuable, relevant, and consistent content that attracts and retains a clearly defined audience. This can be in the form of blog posts, articles, newsletters, or even videos. The goal of content marketing is to establish your business as a thought leader in the quail industry and to educate potential customers about the benefits of your products.

In addition to social media and content marketing, you can also use more traditional methods such as print ads, radio commercials, and television commercials to reach your target market. While these methods may be more expensive, they can still be effective in certain situations.

As you market your quail products, it is important to establish your brand and differentiate yourself from the competition. This can be done through packaging, branding, and storytelling. Consider using unique packaging that stands out on store shelves and reflects the values and personality of your brand. Create a brand logo and design a cohesive visual identity that includes colors, typography, and imagery. And use storytelling to communicate the unique story of your business and the passion that goes into creating your quail products.

Finally, it is important to measure and analyze the effectiveness of your marketing efforts. This can be done through the use of tools such as Google Analytics, which allows you to track website traffic and conversion rates. You can also use customer surveys and focus groups to gather feedback and insights. By continually analyzing and adjusting your marketing strategies, you can optimize your efforts and achieve maximum results.

Marketing your quail products can be a challenging but rewarding task. By understanding your target market, utilizing social media and content marketing, establishing your brand, and measuring and analyzing your efforts, you can effectively market your quail products and grow your business.

CHAPTER FIFTEEN

TIPS AND TRICKS FOR SUCCESSFUL QUAIL FARMING

Choose the right breed of quail for your operation. Different quail breeds have different characteristics, such as egg production, meat production, and hardiness. Some popular quail breeds for egg production include the Japanese quail and the Bobwhite quail, while the Coturnix quail is a popular choice for meat production. Research the various breeds and choose one that fits your goals and climate. Consider factors such as the amount of space you have available, the climate in your area, and the end use of the quail (e.g. egg production, meat production, show, etc.).

Set up a suitable habitat for your quail. Quail need a clean, well-ventilated space with plenty of room to move around. A good rule of thumb is to provide at least 3-4 square feet of space per quail. The enclosure should also have perches, nesting boxes, and a dust bath area. The perches and nesting boxes should be placed at different heights to provide a sense of security for the quail. The dust bath area should be a shallow container filled with sand or dirt, which the quail can use to clean their feathers and keep parasites at bay.

Provide a balanced diet for your quail. Quail need a diet that is high in protein and calcium to support egg production and healthy feather growth. A commercial quail feed can provide all the nutrients they need, but you can also supplement with scraps from the kitchen, such as vegetables and grains. Be sure to offer a variety of foods to ensure that the quail are getting all the nutrients they need. Fresh, clean water should be available at all times.

Keep the enclosure clean and well-maintained. Quail produce a lot of waste, so it's important to keep the enclosure clean to prevent the buildup of harmful bacteria. Regularly clean out the bedding, perches, and nesting boxes, and replace them as needed. The bedding should be changed every 1-2 weeks, or more frequently if it becomes soiled. The perches and nesting boxes should be disinfected every few weeks to prevent the buildup of bacteria and parasites.

Monitor the health of your quail. Keep an eye out for signs of illness, such as weight loss, lethargy, and respiratory issues. If you notice any of these signs, isolate the affected quail and seek the advice of a veterinarian. Regularly check the quail for parasites, such as mites and lice, and treat as necessary.

Practice biosecurity measures to prevent the spread of disease. This includes separating new quail from the rest of the flock until they have been properly quarantined, disinfecting the enclosure and equipment regularly, and preventing contact with wild birds. Use separate equipment for new quail, and disinfect it after use to prevent the spread of disease. Avoid introducing new quail to the flock if there is an outbreak of disease, and isolate any sick quail to prevent the spread of illness.

Provide proper lighting for your quail. Quail need a consistent light cycle to maintain their egg production. A light cycle of 14-16 hours of light per day is ideal. Use a timer to turn the lights on and off at the same time each day.

Plan for the changing seasons. Quail need additional lighting and heat in the winter months to maintain their egg production. Make sure you have a plan in place to provide these necessities as the weather gets colder. This may include adding heat lamps or heat pads to the enclosure, or insulating the coop to retain heat. Make sure the quail have access to a source of light during the shorter days of winter, as well as a source of heat if necessary. In the summer months, make sure the quail have access to shade and ventilation to keep them cool.

Consider adding a predator-proof fence to your enclosure. Quail are vulnerable to predators such as cats, dogs, and raccoons. Adding a fence can help protect your flock and keep them safe. Make sure the fence is high enough to prevent predators from jumping over, and use a mesh with small enough holes to prevent them from reaching through.

Stay up to date on the latest quail farming techniques and technologies. The world of quail farming is constantly evolving, and staying informed can help you stay ahead of the curve and improve the success of your operation. Attend workshops and seminars, join a quail farming group or association, and read industry publications to stay informed.

MEMORABLE QUOTE

"If you are considering starting a quail farm, there are a few things you should know. First, quail farming requires a relatively small investment compared to other types of poultry farming. Quail can be raised in small spaces, such as a backyard or a small farm, and they do not require expensive housing or equipment"

THANK YOU

I wanted to take a moment to express my gratitude for reading this book to its conclusion. It means a lot to me that you took the time and effort to delve into the subject matter and complete the book.

Your dedication and commitment to learning more about quails is truly admirable, and I appreciate the interest you have shown in this topic. I hope that the book has provided you with valuable insights and knowledge about these fascinating birds.

THE END

Printed in the USA
CPSIA information can be obtained
at www.ICGtesting.com
LVHW041557141124
796653LV00010B/133